NATIONAL GEOGRAPHIC

LADDERS

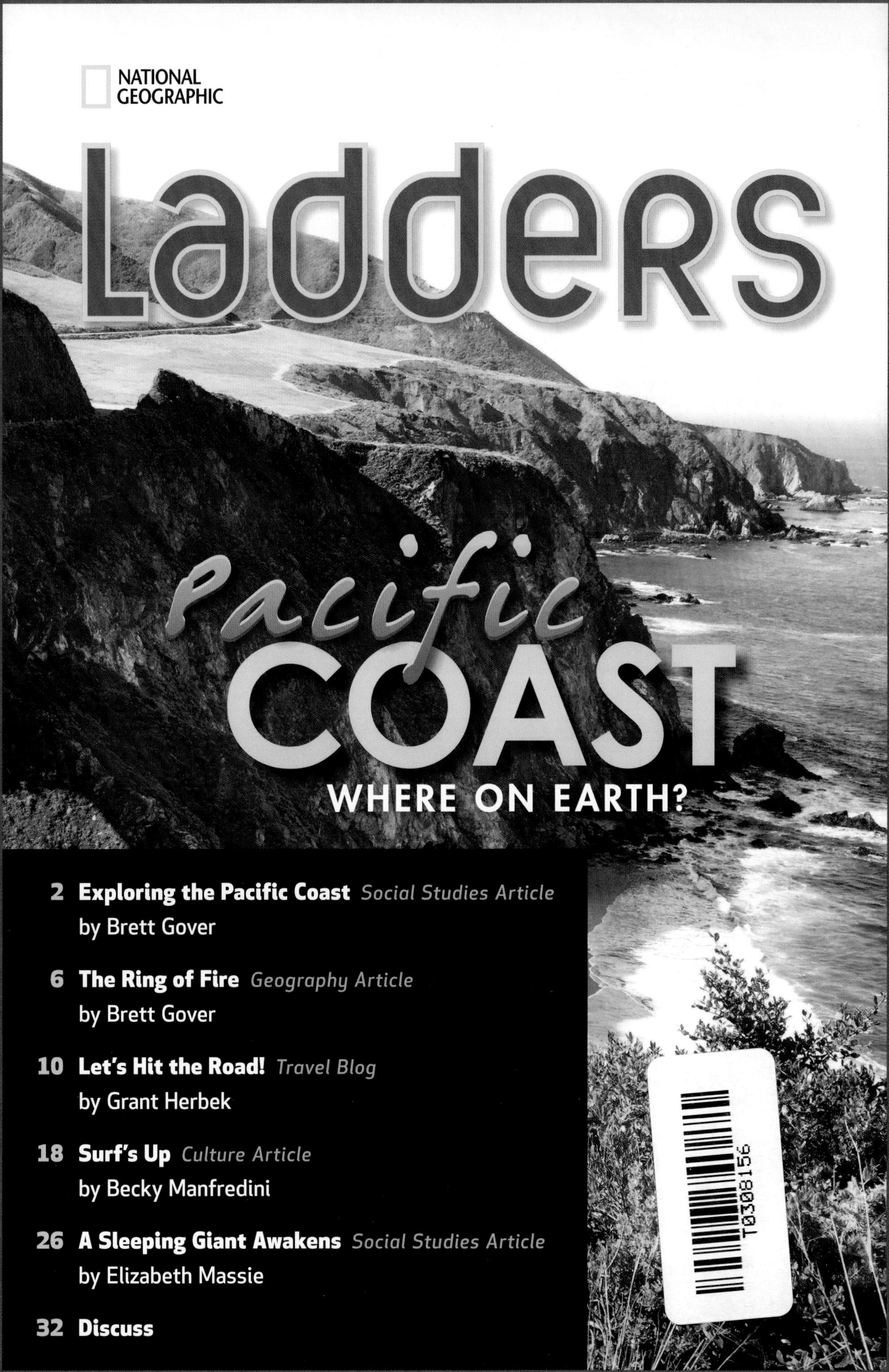

Pacific COAST

WHERE ON EARTH?

GENRE Social Studies Article

Read to find out about the geography of the Pacific coast.

EXPLORING THE PACIFIC COAST

by Brett Gover

It has sunny beaches and giant redwoods in California. It has **glaciers**—large sheets of ice—in Alaska, and **volcanoes** in Hawaii. The Pacific coast has it all.

This diverse region borders the Pacific Ocean, the world's largest ocean. The Pacific coast spans several thousand miles and includes Alaska, Washington, Oregon, and California. The Pacific coast also includes the eight main islands of Hawaii. Hawaii lies more than 2,000 miles from California, in the middle of the Pacific Ocean.

Most major **earthquakes** and most volcanic eruptions in the United States occur along the Pacific coast. An earthquake is a violent shaking of Earth's surface. A volcano is an opening in Earth's crust where melted rock and gases escape from underground. Despite these hazards, many people live on the Pacific coast. The same **geological** forces that cause earthquakes also create beautiful landscapes.

Many people go whale and dolphin watching along the Pacific coast. They will see sights like this humpback whale back-flipping into the water. When a whale jumps out of the water it is called breaching.

Where on Earth?

THE PACIFIC COAST

The five states along the Pacific coast have rich histories and spectacular natural features. Check out these facts.

California

Redwood trees in the forests of California are the tallest trees in the world. The tallest redwood soars to about 365 feet. That's the height of a 30-story building!

Alaska

The sun sends particles, or tiny bits of matter, into space. When these particles hit the gases in Earth's atmosphere, they create colorful lights that can be seen in the night sky of Alaska. We call these the northern lights.

Hawaii

The Hawaiian Islands are actually the tops of volcanoes rising from the ocean floor. Hawaii's Mauna Loa is the world's largest volcano. Its neighbor, Kilauea, has been erupting since 1983.

Washington

Washington's official state gem is petrified wood—wood that has turned into stone. Dead trees fell and were buried under layers of dirt and rock. Over millions of years, the wood was replaced by minerals, turning it into a fossil.

Oregon

Sea lions, whales, and birds gather at Sea Lion Cave in Florence, Oregon. This natural sea cave is as large as a football field. Can you tell the difference between a sea lion and a seal? Part of a sea lion's ear is on the outside of its body. A seal does not have visible ears.

Check In What are some things that all five states along the Pacific coast have in common?

GENRE Geography Article

Read to find out about the Ring of Fire.

THE RING OF FIRE

by Brett Gover

You're in your room reading when you hear a low rumbling sound. As it grows louder, the floor begins to shake. A vase on your desk topples over. You try to stand, but the shaking jostles you back into your chair. The ground doesn't seem very solid. A few seconds later, the violent shaking stops. You have just experienced an earthquake.

Earthquakes can happen at any time on the Pacific coast—almost daily! Most of them are too small to feel, though. Most of the world's earthquakes and volcanic eruptions occur along the Ring of Fire. The Ring of Fire is an area of land about 25,000 miles long. It's horseshoe-shaped and surrounds the Pacific Ocean. In the Ring of Fire, the earth shakes and volcanoes explode on a regular basis.

In March 2009, Alaska's ice-covered Mount Redoubt erupted. A column of ash shot more than 10 miles up into the sky. The eruption lasted for two weeks.

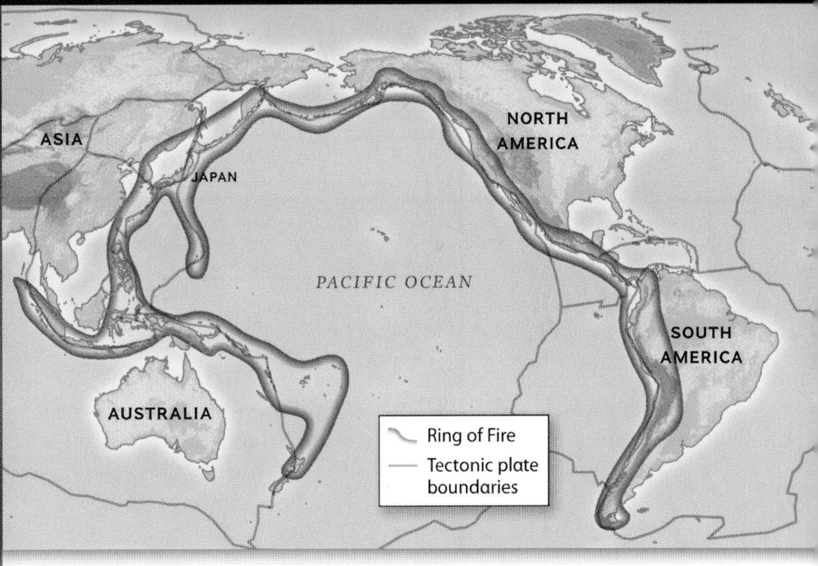

The Ring of Fire follows the coastline of the Pacific Ocean. Read about Earth's plates on the next page.

EARTH IN MOTION

Why do earthquakes and volcanic eruptions occur in the Ring of Fire? Earth's outer layer, or crust, is made up of pieces called **plates**. Many of these plates meet deep underground in the Ring of Fire. On Earth's surface, large cracks called **faults** can form, showing us where the plates meet.

The plates move slowly—only a few inches each year. As a plate moves, its edge can push against another plate. As one plate sinks beneath another, heat underground melts the lower plate. This forms molten, or hot, melted, rock. The molten rock rises up toward the surface of Earth. If it reaches the surface, it can erupt, forming a volcano.

Carrizo Plain, California The San Andreas Fault is where the Pacific and North American plates meet. It is about 800 miles long. When it shifts, it causes both large and small earthquakes.

Sometimes, the edges of plates lock together. They press tighter and tighter against each other. Pressure builds until the plates shift quickly along a fault line, causing an earthquake. If an earthquake occurs beneath the ocean, the plates shifting underwater can create a huge wave called a **tsunami** (soo-NAH-mee). Tsunamis can be far more destructive than the earthquakes that cause them.

In 2011, a powerful underwater earthquake in Japan produced tsunamis that slammed into the land and coastal cities. Giant waves, some more than 30 feet tall, wiped out towns and killed thousands. They also damaged nuclear power plants, causing the release of **radiation**. Japan is still recovering from the disaster.

Tokyo, Japan In 2011, a powerful tsunami toppled many homes and businesses on the coast of Japan.

Northridge, California Earthquakes can cause tremendous damage. A powerful earthquake destroyed thousands of buildings in Southern California in 1994.

Check In What is the Ring of Fire, and where is it?

GENRE **Travel Blog**

Read to find out about different places to visit along California's Pacific coast.

Let's Hit the Road!

by Grant Herbek

I was riding in our SUV with my family when I started this blog. I wanted to document our road trip up California Highway 1. We started near Big Sur and then visited Point Lobos, Monterey, and Pacific Grove. The next day we drove to San Francisco and crossed the Golden Gate Bridge to check out Muir Woods. And finally, we drove inland to gold country. My little brother, Will, couldn't wait to go panning for gold and strike it rich. (Yeah, right.)

On the way to Big Sur, I managed to type blog entries without getting carsick on the twisty coastal highway. We stopped at some amazing overlooks. Hundreds of feet below us, waves crashed against black, jagged rocks. No sandy beaches there, and definitely no surfing for a beginner like me.

At Point Lobos State Reserve, ocean waves carved strange shapes and swirls into this sandstone. It looks soft, like regular sand, but it is hard and rough like stone. We climbed all over it.

Point Lobos

Near Big Sur, we visited Point Lobos State Reserve. A state reserve is an area that's protected from people who'd want to develop the land. In other words, people like miners and builders. Point Lobos used to be called "Point of the Sea Wolves." But we didn't find any wolves there. Instead, we saw tons of barking sea lions. They looked like gray blobs. Sea lions are everywhere along the California coast!

Will kept looking through my binoculars, which was annoying, but then he spotted a water spout in the ocean. I grabbed the binoculars to look for gray whales. But all I saw was a seagull. Our brochure said that every year, gray whales **migrate** 7,000 miles from Mexico to Alaska and back again. Sometimes they stop in this area, so I thought maybe we'd catch a glimpse of them. Next time, maybe.

At Big Sur, the waves kept filling this tide pool with water while we checked it out. There were hermit crabs, starfish, and anemones, which look like plants.

Point Lobos was full of birds. Near a place called Bird Island, Will kept screeching at a black bird called an oystercatcher. It screeched right back at him!

We spent a lot of time climbing the rocks in Pacific Grove and Monterey Bay, looking for cool rocks for Will's collection.

Pacific Grove

From Point Lobos, we drove to Lovers Point Park in the town of Pacific Grove. We grabbed some ice cream and walked along a path that runs along the coastline. Scuba divers were suiting up for a dive on the beach. We talked to them and found out that they hoped to see otters, starfish, and maybe even some rays, which are these really flat fish that are related to sharks. I'd like to try scuba diving some day, but maybe in warmer water.

The ocean along Pacific Grove was full of kayakers. They paddled in calm **inlets** where the waves were small. Huge pieces of sea plants called **kelp** had washed up all along the shoreline. It smelled really bad. The kayakers probably got their paddles tangled in it. At the end of our walk, the wind picked up and the water got choppy. I hope the paddlers made it in safely!

What can dance and glow but has a mean sting? Jellyfish like these. We saw jellyfish in all colors, shapes, and sizes at the Monterey Bay Aquarium.

The sea lions in Monterey Bay were really loud. These young ones were fun to watch. They kept trying to knock each other off the rocks!

Monterey Bay

My mom wanted to visit the Monterey Bay Aquarium, so we stopped there. I have to say, it was worth it. There were so many things to see. Will's favorite was the ray touch tank, where we could put our hands in the water to touch the rays. We saw them flap their fins to find clams in the sand, which was cool.

I liked the three-story kelp forest. It was feeding time when we got there, and a scuba diver swam in the tank and fed the sharks and other fish by hand. It was awesome.

San Francisco

The Monterey Bay Aquarium was my favorite part of our road trip—until I saw San Francisco. What a city! We did a lot there, but I still want to go back to do more.

We started our visit by biking across the Golden Gate Bridge. Did you know that it was painted orange so it could be seen in the fog?

Most days it's overcast in San Fran. Luckily, we had a sunny day for our bike ride, although it got chilly as we crossed the bridge. After crossing the Golden Gate, we ate lunch in a town called Sausalito. We took a ferryboat back to San Francisco instead of biking eight miles back. This was fine with me. My legs felt like rubber after all of that pedaling up and down. San Francisco is a hilly city.

After an earthquake in 1989, sea lions took over a dock at San Francisco's Pier 39. At one point, more than 1,700 sea lions lived there. It is still home to hundreds of sea lions. It was fun to watch them. There's also a webcam of the sea lions online so you can watch them from home.

It took about four years to build the Golden Gate Bridge. It's more than a mile and a half long.

Alcatraz is an old prison. It was built in the middle of the San Francisco Bay so the prisoners couldn't escape. Alcatraz isn't used as a prison anymore, but you can tour it. We did the spooky night tour. I snapped this picture of the creepy prison hospital. I swear it's haunted.

After walking around San Fran, we hopped on a cable car. We checked out North Beach and Chinatown this way. North Beach is an Italian neighborhood with great food, but no beach.

Muir Woods

Muir Woods was named after John Muir, this guy who helped create the U.S. National Park System more than 100 years ago. It's a redwood forest just 11 miles north of the Golden Gate Bridge. I gave my dad directions using my map of California.

Muir Woods was incredible. Redwoods stretch hundreds of feet up. We felt like tiny ants standing next to their trunks. Many of these trees are 600 to 800 years old. One is more than 1,200 years old! We did the two-mile hike so we could see a lot of the forest. It was quiet, chilly, and shady in there.

Coastal redwoods are the tallest living things on Earth. The trees at Muir Woods are around 250 feet tall. Some redwoods grow to be more than 350 feet tall.

Gold Country

Finally it was time to let Will pan for gold. We headed away from the California coast and toward the mountains. After a few hours, we reached Marshall Gold Discovery State Historic Park in Coloma, California. We bought a few gold pans at the gift shop, and the cashier told us that a big discovery of gold in this spot helped start the 1849 California gold rush. Will got even more excited.

After visiting the gold mining museum, we walked down to the American River, where the forty-niners panned long ago. These miners got their nickname from 1849, the year of the gold rush. We swirled water, sand, and little flecks of gold around in our pans, picking out the gold. Dad told me it was probably just pyrite, or "fool's gold," but we didn't tell Will. Striking it rich (sort of) was the perfect end to our road trip.

Will must have filled his pan up a thousand times that day. He would shake it left and right so that the heavy gold would move to the bottom.

My dad loves taking goofy pictures. We couldn't help ourselves when we spotted this tree along the hiking path in Muir Woods.

Check In What's your favorite spot that the blogger wrote about? How would you describe that spot to a friend?

GENRE Culture Article

Read to find out about surfing and its history.

SURF'S UP

by Becky Manfredini

In the Hawaiian language, *he'e nalu* means "to ride the waves." That's just what these surfers are doing in Hawaii.

I'm flying. I'm a bird floating on the wind. I'm one with the wave.

These sentences describe a sport and a way of life—surfing. Many surfers along the Pacific coast say that "catching a wave" and riding it to shore is unlike any other feeling.

Surfing has its **origins**, or beginnings, in Hawaii. In the 1700s, it was considered "the sport of kings." Hawaiian chiefs rode waves to shore by standing on boards up to 24 feet long.

Royal Hawaiian boards could weigh up to 175 pounds and were made of the finest wood. Chiefs would swim out into the ocean and challenge the waves to show their courage. In Hawaiian society, **royalty** surfed in their own coves and reefs. It was forbidden for regular people to ride the same waves as royalty.

Surfing Spots

To find the best waves, experienced surfers study the shoreline and the direction of the waves. They avoid rocky areas and look for quieter, less populated places. Many seasoned surfers are picky about where they surf! Here are a few beaches that meet their high standards:

- **Waikiki (WY-kee-kee) Beach is on the Hawaiian island of Oahu (oh-AH-hoo). It is very popular, so it's often crowded. But if you're a surfing "newbie," Waikiki is a great place to learn.**

Surfrider Beach, in Southern California, became famous after it was in surf films and in songs by a band called the Beach Boys. It's still one of the world's top surfing spots.

- On Oahu's north shore, the Banzai Pipeline challenges even the best surfers with giant, barrel-shaped waves. You'll take a thrilling ride within the "pipeline," or the hollow curl of the wave.

- If you want to surf a mountain, try Mavericks in Half Moon Bay, California. Its tall waves build for as much as a mile before they break, or spill forward. That's when surfers can ride the wave. Each year, Mavericks has a contest where surfers ride dangerous 50-foot waves while trying to avoid rocks and rough seas.

^ A surfer enjoys an exciting ride at Surfrider Beach in California.

< This monster wave is so big they call it Jaws! It can grow as tall as 120 feet. Jaws is located on the Hawaiian island of Maui.

Surfer Gear

What kind of gear do surfers need? It depends on what they want to do. Longboards are usually around nine feet long. It's easy to catch a wave on a longboard because it is very stable. Shortboards are harder for beginners, but experienced surfers like them because they are light and easy to handle. When surfers want to perform tricks, they choose a five- to seven-foot shortboard.

Some people surf without any board. This is called bodysurfing. Bodysurfers wear flippers on their feet to paddle through the water and use their bodies like surfboards. Some say bodysurfing is the ultimate way to connect with the ocean.

What about other gear? In the warm waters of Hawaii, you won't need more than a swimsuit, but in northern California, you'll want to wear a wetsuit. A small amount of water gets trapped between this tight-fitting rubber suit and your body. The water warms to your body's temperature, allowing you to surf in cold water.

Long ago, Hawaiians carved boards out of hardwoods such as mahogany. Today, most surfboards are made of plastic-based materials.

How to Speak Surf

If you're around surfers, you might hear something like this: "Dude, that wave was so *gnarly* that I almost got *rag dolled*! That was *da kine*, but now I need to *chillax*." Many surfers use lots of **slang**.

Why do surfers use made-up words? Just like you and your friends have jokes that only you get, surfers use surf slang to describe experiences they have had in the water. The words can come from anywhere. They are often invented by one person and then spread to the whole community. Here are a few words to get you talking like a real surfer.

Duck Dive

forcing your board underwater, diving beneath a wave, and emerging out the other side

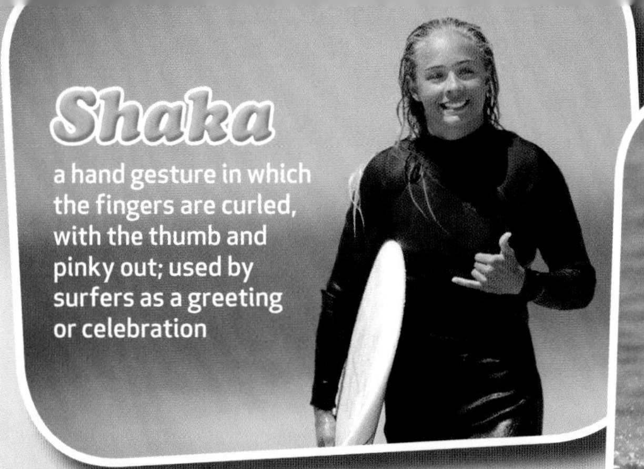

Shaka

a hand gesture in which the fingers are curled, with the thumb and pinky out; used by surfers as a greeting or celebration

Hang Ten

a surfing trick in which the board is steady enough atop the wave that the surfer can hang all ten toes off the nose of the board

Wipeout

falling off the surfboard

Barrel

the hollow tube of a breaking wave

CARVE turning as you ride a wave

CHILLAX a mix between chilling and relaxing

COWABUNGA! an exclamation like "Woo-hoo!" that shows you are having a great time

DA KINE in Hawaiian, this means "the best"

GNARLY cool, even beyond extreme or radical

RAG DOLLED to get thrown or tumbled around by a wave

SHRED to do multiple turns on a shortboard

Check In How are shortboards different from longboards, and why would surfers prefer one over the other?

GENRE Social Studies Article

Read to find out about the eruption of Mount St. Helens and its effects.

A SLEEPING GIANT

A scientist observes a bulge on part of the mountain about a month before the eruption. Rising magma caused the bulge.

RUMBLE, RATTLE, CRACKLE, BOOM!

To most residents, Washington's Mount St. Helens was a sleeping giant. The volcano had not erupted in 120 years. Hikers and photographers were drawn to the beautiful mountain, and many people lived at its base. It rose above

Mount St. Helens is one of 37 volcanoes in the Cascade Mountain range. The Cascades extend more than 700 miles through California, Oregon, Washington, and Canada.

Awakens

by Elizabeth Massie

lush forests filled with bears and elk and was surrounded by sparkling lakes.

But in the spring of 1980, a series of earthquakes began to disturb Mount St. Helens. Cracks began to form in Earth's crust and pressure began to build. The volcano was about to blow.

Before a volcano erupts, **magma**, or melted rock, lurks deep inside it. When pressure inside Earth becomes strong enough, this trapped magma can erupt. It turns into **lava** as it reaches Earth's surface. People knew Mount St. Helens would erupt one day. They just didn't know when it would happen.

Before May 1980, Mount St. Helens stood 9,677 feet above sea level. The eruption blasted away 1,314 feet of the mountain. This made it shorter and rounder.

A VIOLENT ERUPTION

For two months, steam spurted through cracks in the surface of Mount St. Helens. A bulge appeared on one side of the mountain as magma rose inside. The pressure was building. State police tried to evacuate everyone from the area, but some people refused, and tourists kept coming.

On May 18, 1980, an earthquake triggered a landslide along the north side of the mountain. Then a blast blew off that side of the mountain. This exposed the magma and uncorked all of that pressure. More explosions blew ash, gases, rocks, and steam out at a speed of about 300 miles per hour.

A landslide swept down the mountain and buried the area. Hot rocks and ash rained down on the forests and lakes. Ash darkened the sky 250 miles away.

8:32 A.M. The earthquake triggers a landslide. This allows explosive gases and magma to escape from the volcano.

8:32 A.M. Landslides and explosions continue as the side of the volcano blows off.

8:33 A.M. Less than a minute after the landslide, the sky fills with hot gases and billowing clouds of ash.

The eruption killed 57 people and destroyed more than 200 homes. The lava, ash, and mud buried about 200 square miles of land. Many animals and plants were burned, and trees were knocked flat.

"It quickly became as dark as night, yet it was still early afternoon," recalled a local resident. "Even in the short dash from the car to the house, the hot gusts of ash plastered our hair, skin, and clothes with gritty, gray particles."

Rowe Findley, a writer for *National Geographic*, recalled, "As soon as I can, I get airborne for a better look, and recoil from accepting what I see. The whole top of the mountain is gone."

RISING FROM THE ASH

The blast demolished the forests around Mount St. Helens. The **conifers** of the evergreen forests were slow to return. More than 30 years later, these trees still have not fully recovered.

The first plants to come back to the **devastated** area were purple wildflowers called prairie lupines. Gradually, other plants and animals returned. "The eruption really caused drastic changes in the forest ecosystem," said a Washington State University scientist.

Mount St. Helens has not yet entirely calmed down. After the eruption, occasional earthquakes shook the area. In September 2004, the mountain erupted again, although this time the damage was not as bad as in 1980. Still, the eruption kept producing lava until January 2008. As the lava reached the surface, it cooled and hardened into a dome of rock. When the eruption ended, the dome was 1,500 feet high! Scientists are not sure why the eruptions lasted so long.

^ Mount St. Helens may look calm in this present-day photograph, but don't be fooled. It is an active volcano and has a destructive history!

Today, the area around Mount St. Helens is home to elk, coyotes, and many other animals. Tourists ride helicopters and hike around the mountain to see how it has renewed itself. But are they in danger? Since the 1980 eruption, scientists have closely studied Mount St. Helens. As they learn more about it, they hope to be better able to predict when it will erupt again and if there is any danger in exploring the restless giant.

Animals like this golden mantled ground squirrel have returned to the area that was devastated by the volcano.

The first plants to come back to the area were wildflowers like these.

Check In Explain how the 2004–2008 eruption of Mount St. Helens differed from the 1980 eruption.

Discuss

1. What connections can you make among the five selections in this book? How do you think the selections are related?

2. Why are there so many earthquakes and volcanic eruptions in the area known as the Ring of Fire?

3. "Let's Hit the Road!" is a firsthand account of a trip to the Pacific coast. How is reading a travel blog different from reading information in your textbook?

4. What are some of the dangers of surfing? What do you think the benefits might be?

5. What else would you like to know about the Pacific coast? How can you find out more about this region?